50 THINGS YOU SHOULD KNOW ABOUT FOOTBALL

Aidan Radnedge

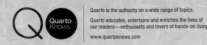

Design and Editorial: Tall Tree Ltd
Project Editor: Harriet Stone
Consultant: Keir Radnedge

© 2018 Quarto Publishing plc

First published in 2018
by QED Publishing
an imprint of The Quarto Group
The Old Brewery, 6 Blundell Street
London, N7 9BH, United Kingdom
T (0)20 7700 6700 F (0)20 7700 8066
www.QuartoKnows.com

A catalogue record for this book is
available from the British Library.

ISBN 978 1 78493 280 0

Manufactured in Guangdong,
China CC012018

9 8 7 6 5 4 3 2 1

Words in **bold** are explained
in the glossary on page 78.

CONTENTS

INTRODUCTIO

Football is truly 'the global game'. It is played, watched and loved more than any other sport across the world, from friendly kickabouts in the streets, in playgrounds or on the beach, to cup finals that are watched by hundreds of millions of people worldwide.

CROSSING THE GLOBE

The game was born in England but is now played in virtually every country on Earth. Some 211 different nations entered the qualification competition to reach the 2018 World Cup in Russia, where 32 teams will take part. The 2026 tournament will be the biggest yet, featuring 48 countries. The USA, Canada and Mexico have applied to host the event together – proof of the sport's growing support and success in North and Central America.

▶ Martin Demichelis of Argentina, in blue, leaves German defender Christoph Kramer on the ground during the 2014 World Cup Final in Brazil. Germany won the game 1–0.

THE FANS

Football would be nothing without the fans. They provide the atmosphere as they cheer on their team to victory. The official world record attendance was set in 1950 when 173,850 fans packed the Maracanã stadium in Brazil to watch Brazil lose to Uruguay in the World Cup.

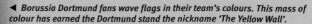

◀ Borussia Dortmund fans wave flags in their team's colours. This mass of colour has earned the Dortmund stand the nickname 'The Yellow Wall'.

4

▲ Football is a sport that can be played anywhere, as shown by these Iranian children playing in a narrow street.

GROWING POPULARITY

From a game initially only played in Britain's schools and universities in the middle of the 19th century, football is now the world's most popular sport. According to football's world governing body, FIFA, some 265 million people play the sport around the globe, 26 million of whom are female, showing how the women's game has grown in popularity.

FOOTBALL INSPIRES

Pelé, possibly the greatest player of all time, refers to football simply as "the beautiful game". Nobel Prize-winning writer Albert Camus declared: "All that I know most surely about morality and obligations, I owe to football". Multiple cup-winning Italian coach Carlo Ancelotti summed up the emotional impact the game has on fans and players when he suggested: "Football is the most important of the less important things in life".

► Pelé played for Brazil from 1957 to 1971, appearing 92 times for his country and scoring 77 goals.

The history of football

Football as we know it today began in the 19th century, but similar games were played thousands of years ago. In China, from 200 BCE, there was a pastime called *cuju*, which involved kicking a ball into a net and was often played inside the emperor's palace. Players were allowed to use any part of the body except their hands. In ancient Japan, people played a similar game called *kemari*.

ANCIENT FORMS

Many early forms of football allowed players to use their hands as well as their feet to control and move the ball. These included *episkyros* in ancient Greece, the Roman Empire's *harpastum*, *chuk-guk* in Korea and *woggabalari* in Australia. Some surviving documents from medieval England refer to "the foot-ball game" in which players kicked the ball – and also each other. The Elizabethan playwright William Shakespeare mentions the game in the plays *King Lear* and *The Comedy of Errors*.

◀ *An ancient Greek athlete balances a ball on his thigh on this gravestone dating from 400 BCE.*

KEY EVENTS

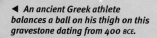

200 BCE
Evidence of an ancient Chinese ball game called *cuju* exists. It is recognized as the earliest form of football (see page 6).

1848
The Cambridge Rules are drawn up at Cambridge University. They allow forward passes and forbid running while holding the ball (see page 8).

1863
The Football Association is formed in England, and becomes the first governing body of association football (see page 8).

▼ This early football game was played on the street in Kingston upon Thames, London, and shows just how violent mob football could be.

DANGEROUS GAMES

From the 11th century onwards, another early form of football played in England involved two large teams who tried to get a ball from one end of their town or village to the other in any way they could, often causing injuries. It was known to some as 'mob football', and King Edward III banned the sport in 1363.

WHAT'S IN A NAME?

The word **'soccer'** is said to have been invented by Englishman Charles Wreford Brown as an abbreviation of 'association football'. Wreford Brown played for Corinthian FC, a club that was strictly for amateur players only, and also captained early England teams. The term 'soccer' is now chiefly used in the US to distinguish it from American football.

▶ Charles Wreford Brown was also a talented cricketer.

1872
The FA Cup is held for the first time. Wanderers beats the Royal Engineers in the final, held at the Kennington Oval in London (see page 9).

1939
Players regularly start to wear numbers on their shirts to show their position and to help spectators tell them apart (see page 13).

1970
The World Cup in Mexico is the first tournament to be broadcast live on television in colour. It is won by Brazil (see page 12).

How it all began

As football games became more popular, people developed their own rules and laws, which led to confusion when some teams played each other. In the 1860s, a group of teams and players decided to lay out one set of the laws, creating the sport of 'association football'. Other forms of football continued to develop, creating the different types, or codes, that are played around the world today.

▲ Gaelic football is a code that was developed in Ireland in the 19th century.

LEARNING THE GAME

One of the earliest sets of football rules, the Cambridge Rules were drawn up by schools including Eton and Harrow in 1848. Ebenezer Cobb Morley, a lawyer from Hull, wrote the first official 'Laws of the Game' in 1862. The world's first Football Association was formed in August 1863 at the Freemasons' Tavern public house in London.

▼ In 1859, Australian rules football became the first football game to set an official code.

RIVAL CODES

In many of the early codes of football, players were allowed to catch and run with the ball. The version of the game played at Rugby School, England, developed into rugby football, which later split into two codes: rugby league and rugby union. The game of American football was developed at US universities from a version of rugby, while Australian rules football became popular in Australia as a way to keep cricketers fit in the winter.

◄ In rugby football, the ball can be carried and passes must be made backwards.

Spreading the word

With one agreed set of rules, association football spread around the globe. British workers travelled abroad and found plenty of people keen to get involved in this new game. Just a few decades after the first competition in England had been established, major international federations and tournaments had been launched all around the world.

KNOCK-OUT CUP

One of the world's first cup competitions, the FA Cup, was held in England in 1872, 16 years before the formation of the first league. Teams play in rounds of knock-out games before two sides face each other in a final. Many of the FA Cup's first winners were amateur teams, including its earliest winners Wanderers, Old Etonians and Oxford University. Later, professional town and city clubs came to dominate. North London club Arsenal is the most successful team in the competition and has won the trophy 13 times.

▲ The original FA Cup was stolen. It was replaced with this exact replica, which was used between 1896 and 1910.

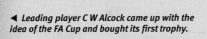

◄ Leading player C W Alcock came up with the idea of the FA Cup and bought its first trophy.

INTO SOUTH AMERICA

British **immigrants** helped to spread the game around the world. A match was played under association rules in Argentina in 1867, and Scottish teacher Alexander Hutton set up the country's first league in 1891. The first league in Brazil was set up by Charles Miller, the son of a Scottish railway engineer, in 1902. Miller had been sent to school in England and returned to Brazil with two footballs and a rulebook.

▲ Charles Miller (front middle) pictured here in 1904 with the team he founded, São Paulo Athletic Club.

Global growth

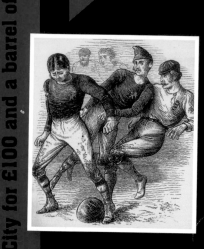

As football spread around the globe, competition between teams from different countries increased, leading to the first international matches. Further demand for the sport drove technological advances such as floodlights, which meant that more matches could be played, causing more and more money to pour into the sport.

◀ *Illustration of the first international match, England vs Scotland, in 1872.*

INTERNATIONAL APPEAL

Teams made up of English and Scottish players faced each other five times in 1870 and 1871, but the first official international match was played between the two countries in Glasgow on 30 November 1872. England was favourite to win, but Scotland held on for a goalless draw. The first international game outside Europe was played in New Jersey, USA, on 28 November 1885, when the host nation was beaten 1–0 by Canada.

WORLD CONTEST

Football was included in the Olympic Games in 1900 but the first official World Cup was held in 1930, followed by tournaments in 1934 and 1938. The first World Cup after World War II, held in Brazil in 1950, was watched by more spectators than any World Cup until the 1994 tournament in the USA.

▲ *A poster from the 1930 World Cup. Uruguay was chosen to host the tournament after its success in some of the early Olympic football tournaments.*

LANDMARK TRANSFERS

▲ *Alf Common, the world's first £1000 footballer.*

£100: Willie Groves
West Bromwich Albion to Aston Villa, 1893

£1000: Alf Common
Sunderland to Middlesbrough, 1905

£152,000: Luis Suárez
Barcelona to Internazionale, 1961

£922,000: Johan Cruyff
Ajax to Barcelona, 1973

£5 million: Diego Maradona
Barcelona to Napoli, 1984

£15 million: Alan Shearer
Blackburn Rovers to Newcastle United, 1996

◀ *Alan Shearer at Newcastle United.*

In 1921, defender Ernie Blenkinsop was bought by Hull City for £100 and a barrel of beer.

10

The first footballers were amateurs, but by the 1930s, most of the major leagues in the world were professional. Today's top players can earn huge amounts of money, with Brazilian star Neymar reportedly earning more than £500,000 a week.

◄ *Brazilian Neymar became the world's most expensive player when he moved to French club Paris Saint-Germain in 2017.*

LIGHTS AND FLIGHTS

Records of matches played under floodlights date back to the 19th century, but they weren't allowed in English league matches until the 1950s. Many clubs started to use them, allowing more matches to be played in the evenings. Advances in air travel made it more attractive for teams to go on foreign tours. Fans were eager to see clubs from different countries face each other in competitions such as the European Cup, which was first held in 1955.

▲ *The first floodlit matches took place at Bramall Lane, Sheffield, in 1878.*

£46.6 million: Zinedine Zidane
Juventus to Real Madrid, 2001

£80 million: Cristiano Ronaldo
Manchester United to Real Madrid, 2009

£86 million: Gareth Bale
Tottenham Hotspur to Real Madrid, 2013

£89 million: Paul Pogba
Juventus to Manchester United, 2016

£145 million: Kylian Mbappé (most expensive teenager ever)
Monaco to Paris Saint-Germain, 2017

£198 million: Neymar
Barcelona to Paris Saint-Germain, 2017

▶ *Paul Pogba, playing for Manchester United in 2017.*

Turning high-tech

▲ *Before a match, the goal-line technology is tested to make sure the cameras are accurate.*

Football remains a simple game, played to the same set of rules in local parks and huge stadiums. However, decision-making in important matches is now done with the help of technology, and games are covered by worldwide media.

GOAL-LINE TECHNOLOGY

There have been many moments of controversy over whether the ball has crossed the **goal line** and a **goal** has been scored. In the 1966 World Cup Final, a goal was given to England against Germany when the ball may not have crossed the line. Today, a system of high-speed cameras tells **referees** whether they can award a goal or not.

VIDEO REPEATS

In 2016, FIFA started testing a new system using video assistant referee (VAR) technology, where television replays are used to make important decisions. The system was first used at the 2016 FIFA Club World Cup in Japan.

▶ *Referee Fabio Maresca consults VAR technology during a match in Italy's Serie A in 2017.*

TELEVISION'S IMPACT

The first major match to be televised was an international between England and Scotland in 1938. Most games were shown in black and white before the 1970 World Cup in Mexico, the first tournament to be shown in colour. Fans can now watch games from around the world every day.

◀ *TV camera crews work at an Asian Cup football game in Australia.*

Caps and numbers

Today's players no longer wear the caps and hats worn by the earliest footballers. And while the earliest shirt numbers showed a player's position, modern players are given a squad number that's theirs to keep.

▲ USA forward Kristine Lilly is the all-time most capped player in the world, having played 354 times for her country.

NUMBERS GAME

Players began to wear numbers on their backs regularly from 1939. The numbers went from 1 to 11 and indicated the player's position, with the goalkeeper wearing 1. Argentina's 1982 World Cup squad wore numbers in alphabetical order, so midfielder Norberto Alonso wore 1. Today, players have squad numbers that may range from 1 to 99.

TOP CAPS

Games played by footballers for their country are referred to as **'caps'**. This tradition began when the first England internationals were awarded a cap for each appearance, with the date and the name of the opponent on them. Egyptian midfielder Ahmed Hassan holds the men's record of 184 caps.

▶ In this Confederations Cup match between Portugal and Mexico in 2017, the players wear the squad numbers given to them for the tournament.

Kristine Lilly scored 130 goals for the USA during her 23-year international career.

The laws of the game

Every game needs to be played according to a set of agreed rules, or laws. They ensure the end result is as fair as possible. The laws of football have been altered many times over the years.

▲ Striker Wayne Rooney takes a penalty kick for Manchester United in a match against AS Roma in 2014.

RULE-MAKERS

The International Football Association Board (IFAB) was set up in 1886 to agree the 'Laws of the Game' to be applied in all matches. These built on the rules that were drawn up in England in 1863. Britain's founding role in creating the laws of the game is still recognized today: the four countries of the United Kingdom (England, Scotland, Northern Ireland and Wales) each have a member of the board, with another four from the rest of the world. At least six members must be in favour of any change in the laws.

PENALTY KICKS

One of the most significant early changes approved by the IFAB came in 1891. It followed an idea apparently first suggested by Northern Irish goalkeeper William McCrum. Defending teams who committed a **foul** in their own **penalty** areas were punished with a penalty kick from 12 yards. The first ever penalty was scored by Scottish player James McLuggage, for Royal Albert against hosts Airdrieonians at Mavisbank Park in Scotland on 6 June 1891.

KEY EVENTS

1886
The International Football Association Board is set up to agree and oversee the laws of football (see page 14).

1891
A goal with a net is introduced into the laws of the game. This follows the introduction of the crossbar 16 years earlier (see page 17).

1904
The Fédération Internationale de Football Association (FIFA) is established to oversee the sport around the globe (see page 18).

THE REF'S IN CHARGE

Referees are responsible for enforcing the laws during a match. They were first made compulsory in England in 1891. Football's world governing body FIFA now has an official list of more than 3000 approved referees for international games. The list is managed by former referee Pierluigi Collina, who was in charge of the 2002 World Cup Final and was named FIFA Referee of the Year six times in a row between 1998 and 2003. Referees used to wear all black but World Cup referees now have a choice of black, blue, green, yellow or red.

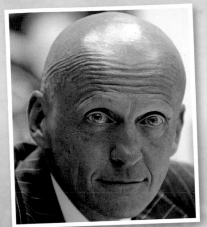

◀ *Italian Pierluigi Collina is widely considered to be one of the best referees of all time.*

▲ *Referees need to be strong-willed to firmly wave away complaints from players.*

NEW IDEAS

One of the IFAB'S most recent meetings in June 2017, led by former English referee David Elleray, suggested that referees could stop their watches at every stoppage and reduce matches from 90 to 60 minutes. The meeting also considered allowing players to pass to themselves at **corners** and **free kicks**. These changes have not yet been agreed, but may be made in the future.

1925
The offside law is changed so that only two rather than three opposition players need to be between an attacker and the goal (see page 19).

1970
Referees use red and yellow cards for the first time at the World Cup in Mexico. The idea came from the colours of traffic lights (see page 19).

1995
The maximum number of substitutes allowed is increased to three. These can be chosen from among a group of squad players (see page 16).

Evolution of the laws

Just 17 laws were included in football's first rulebook in 1863. The laws banned deliberately kicking, tripping or charging other players, and said that only goalkeepers could touch the ball with their hands. New laws have since been added.

EXTRA TIME

Matches last 90 minutes, split into two halves of 45 minutes each. **Extra time** was first introduced in 1897. If the scores are level at the end of a cup tie's 90 minutes, another 30 minutes of extra time can be played. In 1993, some competitions started to use a new 'golden goal' system. This meant that extra time ended as soon as someone scored. Oliver Bierhoff won the 1996 European Championship final for Germany against the Czech Republic with a golden goal. The idea was dropped in 2004, as teams had become very defensive out of fear of conceding the decisive goal.

▶ An official holds up a board with the number of the player to be substituted.

▲ Brazilian reserves sit on the bench during an international match. The three substitutes can be chosen from among a number of the reserves.

SUPER SUBS

Substitutes were introduced for World Cup **qualifiers** in 1954. The first substitute in the World Cup finals was the Soviet Union's Anatoliy Puzach, who came onto the field against Mexico in 1970. Before then, if a player was injured, their team had to carry on without any replacement. Today, up to three changes can be made each game, and players are often substituted for tactical reasons.

Pitch, kit and equipment

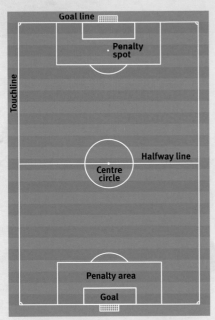

Football's laws state how big a football pitch and the goals should be for a match. They also cover the size and weight of the balls and what players should wear, including the boots on their feet.

SIZE MATTERS

Football pitches measure between 90 metres and 120 metres in length and between 45 metres and 90 metres in width. There is a rectangular penalty area in front of each goal, measuring 40.2 metres by 16.5 metres. Goals are 2.44 metres high and 7.32 metres wide. Crossbars were added for the first time in 1875.

FOOTBALL BOOTS

Early players tended to wear shin-high boots – often the same ones they wore to work in a factory – with nailed-in studs. Boots were usually black, but nowadays players often opt for bright colours. Today's boots are made from modern, lightweight materials and use different types of studs to suit different pitches and conditions.

▲ Modern boots are lightweight and strong but flexible. These boots have moulded studs, which are good for playing on dry pitches.

MATCH BALLS

Early footballs were made of leather and were heavy, especially when they got wet. Today's balls are made of waterproof plastic. Balls must be 68–70 cm in circumference, and weigh 420–445 g.

▲ The ball for the 1934 World Cup was leather with cotton stitches.

▲ A waterproof ball was used for the first time for the 1974 World Cup.

▲ The ball for the 2014 World Cup was designed for accurate shooting.

FIFA

Football's world governing body FIFA, which organizes the World Cup, was founded in Paris on 21 May 1904 at a meeting of representatives from Belgium, Denmark, France, Germany, the Netherlands, Spain, Sweden and Switzerland. Its initials stand for *Fédération Internationale de Football Association*, French for the International Federation of Association Football.

FIFA FINANCE

FIFA hands out grants to national federations to support all levels of the game in each country, from schools, academies and non-league teams to top-division clubs and international matches. FIFA makes most of its money from the World Cup, held every four years, which attracts sponsors from all over the globe.

EXPANSION

Brazil's João Havelange took over the FIFA presidency in 1974 with a promise to expand the game and give more World Cup places to countries outside Europe and South America. To allow for this, the World Cup finals were expanded to include 24 teams in 1982, and 32 teams in 1998. The current president, Gianni Infantino, has promised to expand the World Cup to 48 teams from 2026 onwards.

▶ *Gianni Infantino took over as FIFA president in 2016, replacing fellow Swiss Sepp Blatter.*

▼ *FIFA headquarters located in Zurich, Switzerland. The complex includes offices and a full-size international-standard pitch.*

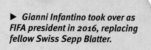

Discipline

The referee is essential to making sure a game is played as fairly as possible. He or she is in charge of starting and ending a game, and giving free kicks when fouls or **handballs** are committed – or awarding penalties if the offence is in a team's own area.

▲ *The assistant referee carries a flag, which she waves to signal to the referee for offside or a foul.*

ASSISTANT REFEREES

Two assistant referees, one on each touchline, help out with decisions, but their main job is spotting **offside**. That means making sure that an attacking player has at least two opponents between them and the goal when the ball is passed forwards to them in the opposition half.

▶ *In big matches, the referee and assistants wear microphones and earpieces so that they can communicate with one another.*

RED AND YELLOW CARDS

Players are shown a yellow card for offences such as a dangerous foul, deliberate handball or arguing with the officials. If they are shown a second yellow card in the same match, they are then shown a **red card** and sent off (ordered to leave the field). A red card can be shown straight away if a player is judged to have been violent or stops a clear goal-scoring chance with a foul or handball. Cards were used for the first time at the 1970 World Cup in Mexico.

▲ *A sending off can have a big effect on a match as one team will have to complete the game with 10 players.*

In the 2006 World Cup, referee Graham Poll showed the same player three yellow cards.

The game's people

Some of the biggest clubs today are worth billions of pounds, have fans around the world that number in the millions, and are covered by TV companies from hundreds of different countries. This is a long way from the early days of football, when clubs were formed by small groups of fans and players.

HUMBLE ORIGINS

The first clubs were formed in England and Scotland in the 19th century. They included teams set up by factories, churches, other sporting clubs such as those playing cricket during the summer, and the schools and universities that agreed the first official rules. Manchester United began as a team called Newton Heath, made up of Lancashire railway workers, while Arsenal started with staff at a weapons-making factory in Woolwich, south London. English clubs that grew out of churches include Merseyside rivals Liverpool and Everton and the West Midlands sides Aston Villa and Wolverhampton Wanderers.

▲ *The Newton Heath team poses for a photograph in 1892. The club changed its name to Manchester United in 1902.*

1902
After running up debts, Newton Heath FC is given fresh investment by local businessmen and changes its name to Manchester United (see page 20).

1930s
Italy achieves consecutive World Cup victories under the guidance of manager Vittorio Pozzo in 1934 and 1938 (see page 22).

1990
Franz Beckenbauer wins the World Cup as manager of West Germany, 16 years after winning it as captain (see page 22).

▲ *Real Madrid plays at the Santiago Bernabéu Stadium, which holds 81,000 people.*

EXPANDING SIDES

Many of today's big clubs were formed by groups of friends who were just keen to play, but they have grown to become enormous businesses. Spanish club Real Madrid is one of the richest clubs in the world. It has almost 100,000 voting members, known as 'socios', who get to choose the club's president. Current president Florentino Pérez won support by promising major **transfers**, and his signings have included stars such as Cristiano Ronaldo, Kaka and Zinedine Zidane.

SCRUTINY AND ANALYSIS

The first football teams tended to play a style of the game that involved the person on the ball **dribbling** for as long as they could, with the rest of the players chasing them to try to win it back. The Scottish international sides of the 1870s were the first to develop a passing game, and teams started to think about tactics and positioning. Today, teams' tactics are studied not only by coaches and their back-up teams but also by TV analysts, who are often former players.

▼ *Television camera crews from around the world capture every second of big matches from many different angles.*

1994
Brazil wins the World Cup held in the USA, led by strikers Romario and Bebeto (see page 27).

2000
Florentino Pérez takes over as Real Madrid president, starting a period in which the club makes a series of big-name signings (see page 21).

2008
Spain wins the European Championships playing a short-passing style of football called tiki-taka, which relies on skilful midfield players (see page 29).

13

▶ Sir Alex Ferguson celebrates winning the 2008 Champions League final.

Managers

The manager is in charge of picking the team, training between matches and deciding what tactics to use. Often the manager will be helped by coaches, fitness experts and scouts who look for potential new players all over the world.

BIG WINNERS

Two managers have won eight different FIFA and UEFA club trophies: Carlo Ancelotti with AC Milan and Real Madrid, and Sir Alex Ferguson with Aberdeen and Manchester United. Vittorio Pozzo is the only person to win the World Cup twice as a manager, leading Italy to victory in 1934 and 1938. Brazil's Mário Zagallo and Germany's Franz Beckenbauer have won the World Cup both as players and as managers.

▲ Jürgen Klinsmann (left) and Franz Beckenbauer both played for and managed the German national side.

SACK RACE

Losing their job is something all managers may have to deal with, even the most successful. Claudio Ranieri was sacked as manager of Leicester City in February 2017, just nine months after winning the English Premier League. However, he survived longer than Leroy Rosenior, who was dismissed by English club Torquay United in May 2007 after just 10 minutes in the job.

▶ Italian Claudio Ranieri led Leicester City to its first league title in 2016, but that did not save his job when the team did badly the following season.

Goalkeepers

Goalkeepers are the only players allowed to use their hands, and only when they are inside their penalty area. Keepers can be their team's hero with a great save, but it can also be a lonely position, as one mistake may lose the game.

▲ *Campos designed this shirt for himself to wear in goal.*

ESSENTIAL INSTINCTS

A goalkeeper's job requires a unique set of skills. They need to be agile enough to make spectacular saves and have the strength of mind to organize the defence in front of them. Increasingly, goalkeepers need to be comfortable dribbling and passing the ball too. Germany's 2014 World Cup winner Manuel Neuer is renowned not only for saving goals but also for starting his own team's attacks with a well-placed pass.

STANDING OUT

Mexico goalkeeper Jorge Campos was a man of many talents. He liked stopping shots, scoring goals and also designing his team's kit, making it as bright and multi-coloured as possible.

◄ *Spain keeper Iker Casillas is nicknamed 'Saint Iker' for his ability to make miraculous saves.*

EYE FOR GOAL

Some goalkeepers enjoy joining the outfield action. Paraguay's José Luis Chilavert used to run into the opposition half to take free kicks. He scored eight times for his country, including a last-minute equalizer against Argentina in a qualifier for the 1998 World Cup.

► *Chilavert had a powerful left foot, and was expert at taking long-range free kicks.*

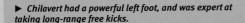

Goalkeeper José Luis Chilavert scored 46 goals for the clubs he played with.

Defenders

Some people say that while goal-scoring strikers will win you football matches, goal-stopping defenders will win you championships. Defenders organize, tackle and do almost anything they can to stop the ball hitting the back of their own net.

FULL BACKS

When association football began in the 19th century, the full backs were the only two defenders in a team. Today, this term is used to describe the two defenders who play on the right and left wings. Many full backs enjoy surging forwards. Brazil's Roberto Carlos liked to shoot from long distance. Germany's Philipp Lahm could play as either right back or left back, while Italy's Paolo Maldini played on the left or in the centre.

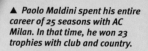

▲ Paolo Maldini spent his entire career of 25 seasons with AC Milan. In that time, he won 23 trophies with club and country.

CENTRE BACKS

Most teams play with two or three players in the centre of defence. Often one of the centre backs will be good at tackling and organizing, while their partner might be more comfortable passing the ball to the midfielders. In the 1960s, Germany's Franz Beckenbauer played as a sweeper, or 'libero', at the back. His job was to break down opposition attacks, then carry the ball forwards to start an attack for his own team.

◄ Franz Beckenbauer played most of his club football for Bayern Munich. As well as being a great tackler and all-round defender, he was famous for setting up dangerous attacks.

Midfielders

As the name suggests, midfielders play in central positions on the field between defence and attack. They need to help out defenders and create chances for forwards, which means they need to have lots of stamina and be very creative.

DEFENSIVE MIDFIELDERS

Defensive midfielders are great tacklers and anticipate danger from their opponents before the ball gets close to their own penalty area. They are fierce competitors who break up attacks and win the ball. The work of defensive midfielders, such as Barcelona and Spain's Sergio Busquets, may go unnoticed, but it is essential to their team's success.

▲ *Barcelona's Sergio Busquets gets past an opponent in a Spanish league match against Sevilla. He is physically strong, but also very skilful and rarely gives the ball away.*

ATTACKING MIDFIELDERS

These are often known as 'playmakers'. They are creative players who can pick out teammates with accurate passes, have the vision to create chances for their strikers and also score their fair share of goals. Spain's Andrés Iniesta would open up the opposition by dribbling past helpless defenders, while France's Zinedine Zidane used his strength and skilful control to create time and space to set up an attack.

◀ *French playmaker Zinedine Zidane scored two goals in the 1998 World Cup Final, in which France beat Brazil 3–0.*

Wingers

Wingers are often the fastest players in a team. They play wide in attack, either on the left or the right side of the pitch, and their main role is to set up goal-scoring chances – although they will often try to score themselves.

NECESSARY SKILLS

Garrincha of Brazil and England's Stanley Matthews, who played in the 1950s and 1960s, were great dribblers of the ball. They would turn one way then another, before racing past a defender with the ball. Crossing the ball is just as important, and England's David Beckham was famous for the accuracy of his crosses. Star strikers Cristiano Ronaldo and Lionel Messi both began their careers playing on the wing.

▶ As well as his ability to run past defenders, Garrincha could shoot powerfully with either foot.

SWITCHING SIDES

Left wingers will often be left-footed and right wingers right-footed, but this is not always the case. Some players prefer to cut in from the side and shoot with their favoured foot at an angle. Bayern Munich won five German league titles in a row between 2012 and 2017, helped largely by two star wingers playing this way – Arjen Robben on the right and Franck Ribéry on the left.

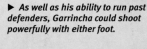

▲ Turkish winger Arda Turan is a right-footer who plays on the left wing for Barcelona.

▶ French midfielder Franck Ribéry started out as a right winger before switching to the left.

In his career, Brazilian winger Garrincha scored four times directly from a corner.

Forwards

Forwards are usually a team's biggest stars, taking the glory for scoring most of the goals. They need to be able to find positions and space from which to shoot, and they also need a calm head in front of goal.

POWER AND SKILL

Centre forwards, or strikers, can use a variety of skills to score goals. Many are big and powerful, such as Ivory Coast's Didier Drogba and Portugal's Cristiano Ronaldo. Others, such as Argentinian Sergio Agüero, are smaller but have the ability to put themselves in the right place at the right time to score.

▲ Didier Drogba uses his physical strength to beat defenders.

▲ Short and powerfully built, Argentina and Manchester City striker Sergio Agüero uses his pace and agility to find space in dangerous positions.

SUPPORT STRIKERS

Two forwards can often be better than one, especially if they work well together. Often, this will be one tall forward and another who is short, quick and able to set up scoring chances. Ukraine's all-time finest strikers Andriy Shevchenko and the smaller Serhiy Rebrov scored 63 international goals between them. Sometimes similar attackers link up well, such as Romario and Bebeto for Brazil in the 1994 World Cup, while Chile's Alexis Sánchez can act as both a goal creator and a goal scorer.

◄ Alexis Sánchez is a versatile striker with two good feet who can play anywhere along the front line.

Australian striker Archie Thompson scored a record 13 goals in one game in 2001.

Skills and tricks

All football players need to learn the basic skills of controlling the ball, passing, shooting and tackling. Some have taken their skills to another level and learnt special tricks. These moves can be used to beat defenders or to shoot from unexpected areas.

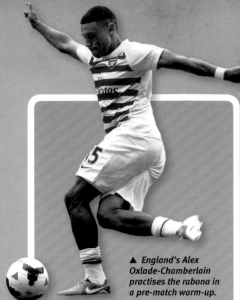

▲ *England's Alex Oxlade-Chamberlain practises the rabona in a pre-match warm-up.*

THE RABONA

The rabona is a skill in which a player kicks the ball around the back of their standing leg. This is a tricky skill to learn, but well worth the practice as it can confuse defenders as to which direction you are intending to kick the ball.

RAINBOW FLICK

Brazilian star Neymar has perfected a number of tricks to bamboozle defences, including the rainbow flick. In this move, he traps the ball between his feet and flicks it into the air by leaping up. The ball loops over his head to land in front of him, with any defenders nearby left stranded.

▲ *Neymar performs a rainbow flick while playing for Brazil.*

BICYCLE KICK

Brazilian forward Leonidas da Silva is said to have invented the bicycle kick in the 1930s, by leaping into the air and shooting the ball backwards over his own head. This spectacular move can be used to shoot at goal or to clear the ball from your own penalty area.

▲ *Spain's Sergio Ramos attempts a shot with a bicycle kick. This shot went just wide. It is hard to hit the target when your back is to the goal like this.*

In 2017, Baroka FC goalkeeper Oscarine Masuluke scored with a last-minute bicycle kick.

Tactics

There are many different ways to play the game, and different tactics have gone in and out of style. Teams come up with successful ideas, then other teams work out how to combat them. Numerical formations show where on the field the players are positioned.

TIKI-TAKA

Tiki-taka is the name given to the quick, short-passing tactics adopted by Barcelona and the Spanish national team in the first decade of the 21st century. It was heavily influenced by the ideas of former Barcelona player and manager Johan Cruyff, and brought huge success to the two teams. This style of play allowed small, skilful midfielders such as Xavi Hernández and Andrés Iniesta to keep the ball and control games.

▲ *Barcelona midfielders Xavi (left) and Iniesta (right) are supremely skilful, and very rarely lose possession.*

POPULAR FORMATIONS

4–4–2 For many teams this is the standard formation, with the two forwards up front either playing close together or one of them dropping back a little closer to midfield.

4-4-2

4–3–3 This used to mean a centre forward with two attacking wingers. Today, the two alongside the central striker often help out in midfield more. This can sometimes look more like a 4–5–1 formation.

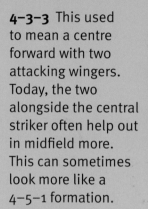

4-3-3

3–4–2–1 Fielding three central defenders can seem a waste if the opposing side only has one striker, but it also allows the full backs to become wing backs with an attacking threat.

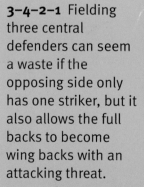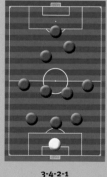

3-4-2-1

TOTAL FOOTBALL

In the 1970s, the Netherlands national team and the club Ajax Amsterdam developed a style dubbed 'Total Football'. It encouraged players to fill in anywhere on the pitch, rather than sticking to their positions as defenders, midfielders or forwards. The style demanded physical fitness, skill and awareness to switch places quickly.

The term 'tiki-taka' was first used by Spanish commentator Andrés Montes in 2006.

The global game

In addition to national leagues, there are also continental cups for clubs and countries as well as global tournaments. The qualifying rounds for these competitions can keep teams busy all year round.

◀ In Australian rules, there are four posts. If the ball passes between the central goalposts, six points are scored. One point is scored if it only passes through the outer posts.

CONCACAF

▼ Map of the world with the six football confederations.

CONMEBOL

THE FIRST CUP

The world's first organized tournament may have been a 12-club contest called the Youdan Cup, held in Sheffield, England, in 1867. Hallam FC beat Norfolk in the final, under an unusual set of rules that awarded 'rouges' as well as goals. Rouges were shots that failed to go through a four-yard-wide goal but were within four yards on either side of that goal. Hallam won the match by two rouges to Norfolk's nil. A similar system is used today in Australian rules football.

KEY EVENTS

1867
The world's first football tournament is held in Sheffield, England, when Hallam FC wins the Youdan Cup (see page 30).

1916
Dick, Kerr's Ladies FC draws a crowd of 52,000 at Goodison Park. A year later, women are banned from playing at English grounds (see page 32).

1977
The first under-20s World Cup is held in Tunisia. The Soviet Union beats Mexico in a penalty shoot-out in the final (see page 34).

WORLDWIDE CUPS

Today, every one of FIFA's member countries has its own league and cup tournament. Clubs from different countries are also involved in continental tournaments, such as the Champions League, and even global competitions, such as the FIFA Club World Cup. On the international stage, the success of the World Cup, which started in 1930, has led to the creation of the **Confederations** Cup, which pits continental champions against each other.

UEFA

CAF

AFC

OFC

▲ Mesut Özil plays for Germany, the current holders of the World Cup and the Confederations Cup.

KEY

CONCACAF: Confederation of North, Central American and Caribbean Association Football

CONMEBOL: Confederación Sudamericana de Fútbol

UEFA: Union of European Football Associations

CAF: Confédération Africaine de Football

AFC: Asian Football Confederation Associations

OFC: Oceania Football Confederation

CONTINENTAL ORGANIZERS

The world of football is divided into confederations. The first, CONMEBOL, was set up for South America in 1916. Confederations for the other continents were founded in the 1950s and 1960s. They organize continental tournaments and qualifying competitions for the World Cup.

1984
Football is played at the Paralympics for the first time, with a seven-a-side game that uses specially adapted rules (see page 34).

2005
The first official Beach Soccer World Cup is held in Rio de Janeiro, Brazil. France beats Portugal in the final (see page 35).

2013
The National Women's Soccer League is founded in the USA. The first season's league winner is Western New York Flash (see page 33).

The women's game

Women's football is on the rise across the world. New professional leagues are being established and TV audiences for major events such as the Women's World Cup are growing enormously. In the USA, female international football players are now often more famous than the male players.

EARLY PIONEERS

In 1920, one of the most popular football teams in the world was made up of women from a munitions factory in Preston, northwest England. The side, known as Dick, Kerr's Ladies FC, was watched by tens of thousands of people, not only in England but also on tours of other countries.

In 1921, however, the Football Association in England announced that it was banning women from playing football in official stadiums. This ban lasted until 1971.

WOMEN'S WORLD CUP

The first FIFA Women's World Cup took place in China in 1991. The USA were the champions, beating Norway 2–1 in the final. The USA also won the 2015 tournament, held in Canada, where it defeated Japan 5–2 in the final. The match was watched by a TV audience of 750 million people.

▼ The Dick, Kerr's Ladies team, pictured here in 1920, was founded in 1917 to raise money for wounded soldiers.

GROWING GAME

Lots of girls play football in US schools and colleges, and there have been several attempts to establish a women's professional league. The most recent, the National Women's Soccer League, began in 2013. It has attracted some of the world's top players, such as Marta from Brazil, Scotland's Kim Little, Canada's Christine Sinclair and Sam Kerr from Australia, as well as US stars such as winger Megan Rapinoe. The most successful team is FC Kansas City, with two league titles.

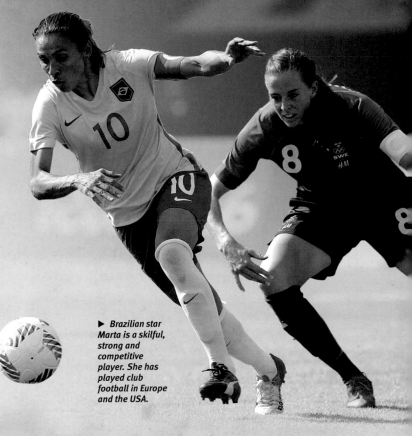

▶ *Brazilian star Marta is a skilful, strong and competitive player. She has played club football in Europe and the USA.*

EUROPEAN CHAMPIONS

The Netherlands hosted the UEFA Women's European Championship in 2017 – and won the tournament for the first time, after beating England 3–0 in the semi-finals and Denmark 4–2 in the final. England's Jodie Taylor was the top scorer with five goals, while Dutch attacker Lieke Martens was voted the tournament's best player. Germany has won the competition a record eight times, including six tournaments in a row between 1995 and 2013.

◀ *Striker Lieke Martens scored for the Netherlands in its win over Denmark in the 2017 European Championships final. She won the Golden Ball as player of the tournament.*

Football for all

Senior professional footballers are not the only ones who get to compete for international trophies. In recent years there have been greater efforts to organize contests for young players, footballers with disabilities and in smaller formats such as five-a-side.

YOUTH OPPORTUNITIES

Global tournaments are held for different age groups, so that the youngest players for clubs and countries are tested at the highest level. The Under-20 World Cup was first held in 1977 in Tunisia, where the Soviet Union beat Mexico in the final. In the 2017 final, England defeated Venezuela 1–0. The Under-17 World Cup was first held in 1985. Current champion Nigeria has won the tournament a record five times.

COMPUTER GAMES

Football video games are now almost as big business as the real thing. In games such as *Football Manager*, you get to coach a team, while other games allow you to control players on the pitch. The FIFA Interactive World Cup is a computer game contest that has been held since 2004. In the 2017 final, England's Spencer Ealing beat Germany's Kai Deo Wollin 7–3.

▲ *In games of blind football, all the players wear masks so that those who are partially sighted do not have an unfair advantage over those who are totally blind.*

PARALYMPICS

Two versions of football are played at the Paralympic Games. Seven-a-side matches for players with cerebral palsy were first added to the Games in 1984. Matches are played over two halves of 30 minutes on small pitches. Five-a-side football for blind or partially sighted footballers was introduced at the Games in 2004. Players follow the ball by listening to a bell inside it.

▼ With a soft surface to land on, beach football players regularly attempt acrobatic moves.

BEACH FOOTBALL

Many Brazilian stars began their careers by kicking a ball about on a beach, and beach football has now become a sport in itself. Teams of five players face each other in games split into three 12-minute sections. Games are fast and furious, with shots taken from all parts of the pitch and an average of 11 goals per match. The first official FIFA Beach Soccer World Cup, held in Brazil in 2005, was won by France. Brazil has been champion five times since then, including the 2017 tournament, when it beat Tahiti 6–0 in the final.

FUTSAL

Futsal is a fast-paced five-a-side game that was developed in South America in the 1930s. Today, there are several professional leagues around the world. The games are normally played indoors on small pitches, which means that players have to develop great close control. The first FIFA Futsal World Cup was held in the Netherlands in 1989, and won by Brazil, which has now won the tournament five times.

▲ Futsal is played on the same pitch and with the same goal as the sport of handball.

The fame game

Football matches attract plenty of famous fans from the world of show business, and sometimes footballers are invited to try their hands as entertainers on the screen as well as on the pitch. Many football stars have been happy to get involved and show they are game for a laugh at the same time.

FAMOUS FANS

Many Hollywood stars support English sides. Tom Hanks supports Aston Villa, Sylvester Stallone has invested in Everton, while movie director Spike Lee and actor Idris Elba cheer on Arsenal. Tennis star Rafael Nadal supports Real Madrid, although his uncle Miguel played for Barcelona. Athlete Usain Bolt has gone one stage further, talking about his desire to play for his favourite club Manchester United.

◄ *Spanish tennis ace Rafa Nadal is one of Real Madrid's many famous fans.*

FOOTBALLING FILMS

David Beckham appeared briefly in the 2002 British comedy film *Bend It Like Beckham*. He appeared at the end of the film, alongside the film's stars Parminder Nagra and Keira Knightley, who play a pair of ambitious young female footballers. *Escape to Victory*, released in 1981, was a film about a football-playing group of Second World War prisoners, and featured not only actors Sylvester Stallone and Michael Caine but also real footballers including Pelé, Bobby Moore and Osvaldo Ardiles.

▶ *Pelé showed off his skills in* Escape to Victory's *climactic clash between a team of prisoners of war and a team of German soldiers.*

Goalkeeper Manuel Neuer was the voice of Frank McCay in the film *Monsters University*.

Mascots

The French word 'mascotte' means 'lucky charm'. Almost every football team now has a mascot, either a real animal or a person dressed in a costume. Their roles include leading the teams out and entertaining and encouraging the supporters both before and during games.

▲ The bald eagle Águia Vitoria flies over the Benfica stadium before landing on the club's crest.

REAL CREATURES

For many years, Finland's lucky mascot was an eagle owl named Bubi that would fly over Helsinki's Olympic Stadium for international matches from 2007 onwards. Benfica in Portugal flies a bald eagle named Águia Vitoria over its Estadio da Luz ground before every home game. German club Cologne has had a series of live goat mascots named after its former player and manager Hennes Weisweiler.

DRESSING UP

People dressed up as mascots have become a familiar sight in football stadiums, especially since the 1980s. A wide variety of costumed creatures can be found, including birds, lions, a whale and even a dinosaur, such as Arsenal's green Gunnersaurus Rex. US club Portland Timbers has a lumberjack who uses a chainsaw to cut a log every time a goal is scored.

◀ Slavek and Slavko, the mascots for the Euro 2012 tournament, dressed in the colours of the host nations Poland and Ukraine.

FIFA, football's governing body, has 211 member countries. Some national sides from Europe or South America have gone down in history as the best ever. Teams from the rest of the world are catching up, and there are now strong teams in every continent.

HUNGARY, 1950s

The Hungary team of the early 1950s was dubbed the 'Magical Magyars'. Back home it was known as the 'Golden Team'. It only lost twice between May 1949 and February 1956, and set a then-world record of 32 games in a row without defeat. The side was widely expected to win the 1954 World Cup but lost to West Germany in the final.

▲ *Ferenc Puskás scored 84 goals in 85 matches for Hungary.*

▲ *The 1970 Brazil side, led from the front by Pelé (on the ball here against Italy), is considered by many to have been the greatest team of all time.*

BRAZIL, 1970

Brazilians call football 'the beautiful game'. Their national team lived up to this description at the 1970 World Cup in Mexico, scoring 19 goals in six games on the way to lifting the trophy. The fourth goal when beating Italy 4–1 in the final included passes between seven different players, ending with the captain, Carlos Alberto, smashing the ball into the net.

Brazil's Jairzinho scored in all six of their games at the 1970 World Cup.

KEY EVENTS

1916
The first South American Championship is held in Buenos Aires, Argentina. The tournament is renamed the Copa América in 1975 (see page 47).

1958
Brazil wins the first of its five World Cups, beating hosts Sweden in the final. The tournament sees the first appearance of a 17-year-old Pelé (see page 41).

1996
Women's football is introduced for the first time at the Olympics. The USA defeats China 2–1 in the final, played in Athens, Georgia (see page 48).

21ST-CENTURY SPAIN

Spain was long seen as one of international football's great underachievers, but won its first World Cup in 2010 thanks to an extra-time goal against the Netherlands by Andrés Iniesta. This came between successive European Championship triumphs in 2008 and 2012. Striker Fernando Torres scored in both European finals: a 1–0 victory over Germany and a 4–0 win over Italy. The team was widely admired for its attacking play, using the 'tiki-taka' short-passing style.

◀ *Fernando Torres was Spain's leading striker during its recent tournament successes.*

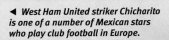

◀ *West Ham United striker Chicharito is one of a number of Mexican stars who play club football in Europe.*

NORTH AND CENTRAL AMERICA

The USA and Mexico dominate this region's competitions, including the CONCACAF Gold Cup, which is held every two years. But their smaller neighbours have also made an impact, including Costa Rica, which reached the quarter-finals of the 2014 World Cup, and qualified again for 2018.

ASIA AND OCEANIA

Australia dominated the Oceania football federation, but left in 2006 to join the Asian equivalent and take on stronger teams such as South Korea and Japan, who jointly hosted the 2002 World Cup. South Korea finished fourth at the 2002 tournament, and has played 30 World Cup finals matches in total – more than any other Asian nation.

AFRICA

Africa hosted its first World Cup in South Africa in 2010, but still awaits its first World Cup semi-finalists. Ghana came close in 2010, losing in the quarter-final against Uruguay in a **penalty shoot-out**. Ghanaian striker Asamoah Gyan missed a penalty in the last minute of extra time that would have won the match. Cameroon and Senegal have also reached the quarter-finals.

◀ *Striker Brown Ideye plays for Nigeria, which has qualified for six out of the last seven World Cup tournaments.*

1997
The first Confederations Cup is held in Saudi Arabia. Brazil beats Australia 6–0 in the final. Ronaldo and Romario both score hat-tricks (see page 49).

2008
Spain wins the European Championship after reaching its first major tournament final in 44 years (see page 41).

2010
The World Cup is held in South Africa, marking the first time the tournament has been hosted by an African country (see page 43).

Major football nations

Although football is a global game, only eight different nations have won the World Cup. A handful of countries consistently set the highest standards and regularly feature in major finals. These nations have enjoyed the greatest success in the top international competitions.

▼ The German team celebrates after winning the 2014 World Cup Final, defeating Argentina 1–0.

GERMANY

Germany has played the most World Cup matches: 106 to Brazil's 104. As West Germany, it lifted the trophy in 1954 and 1974, and then again in 1990, the year East and West Germany reunited. After defeating Argentina in the final in Brazil in 2014, Germany won its fourth World Cup title to go with three European Championships.

SPAIN

Spain won the European Championship in 1964, but this was followed by 40 years of underachievement. Then a stunning Spanish side won three tournaments in a row: the 2008 and 2012 European Championships and the 2010 World Cup. The team featured stars such as midfielders Xavi Hernández and Andrés Iniesta, and strikers David Villa and Fernando Torres.

▲ Xavi Hernández of Spain (left) fights for the ball with Riccardo Montolivo of Italy during the final of the 2012 European Championships. Spain won 4–0.

BRAZIL

Five-time World Cup winner Brazil is famous for a skilful playing style. Many of its most famous players, including Ronaldo, Ronaldinho and Neymar, developed their skills juggling a football on the beach. Brazil legend Pelé is the only player to win three World Cups: in 1958, 1962 and 1970.

▶ Striker Ronaldo was top scorer when Brazil won the World Cup in 1994.

ARGENTINA AND URUGUAY

South American neighbours Uruguay and Argentina have a rivalry that dates back to the 19th century. They met in the first World Cup Final in 1930, which Uruguay won 4–2. Both teams have won the World Cup twice. Uruguay has won the South American championship, known as the Copa América, a record 15 times. Its most recent victory came in 2011, led by Luis Suárez and Edinson Cavani.

▶ Uruguayan striker Luis Suárez is his country's top goalscorer.

ITALY

Italy had a golden period during the 1930s, when it won the World Cup in 1934 and 1938. However, it had to wait until 1982 for its third title, when the team was led by 40-year-old goalkeeper Dino Zoff. Fabio Cannavaro lifted Italy's fourth World Cup in 2006. It failed to qualify for the 2018 finals, missing out for the first time in 60 years. Italy's top division, known as Serie A, is one of the world's most successful leagues.

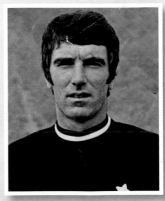

▲ Dino Zoff won the 1968 European Championships with Italy, and lifted the World Cup 14 years later.

Playing host

Hosting a World Cup, or another of football's showpiece tournaments, is a huge honour for a country, but also a great responsibility. Nations that successfully apply must have the cities and the stadiums to cope with welcoming players, officials and thousands of supporters from across the globe.

ENORMOUS STADIUMS

A country may have to construct huge, purpose-built stadiums if it is chosen to host the World Cup finals. Mexico was the first country to stage two World Cup tournaments – first in 1970 and again in 1986 after stepping in to host the tournament when original choice Colombia dropped out. The country's huge Azteca Stadium hosted the finals for both tournaments, and is only the second venue to host two finals, along with Brazil's Maracanã stadium.

▼ The Azteca Stadium in Mexico City holds 87,000 spectators. As well as two World Cups, it also hosted the 1968 Olympic Games football final.

FIRST TIMERS

Uruguay hosted the first-ever World Cup in 1930. Organizers struggled to persuade teams to travel to South America, and only four European countries accepted the invitation to play: Belgium, France, Romania and Yugoslavia. Uruguay remains the smallest country to stage – or win – the tournament.

▲ *Uruguay's victorious 1930 team poses for the cameras.*

AMERICAN WELCOME

The World Cup was held outside Europe and Latin America for the first time in 1994, when the USA was the host nation. The tournament attracted 3.6 million spectators to the matches, more than any tournament before or since. The final, between Brazil and Italy, was watched by 94,194 fans inside the Rose Bowl in Pasadena, California, which later staged the 1999 Women's World Cup Final.

▲ *The Sapporo Dome, Japan, was built for the 2002 World Cup. The pitch is regularly wheeled outside so the grass gets enough sunlight.*

SHARED RESPONSIBILITY

Japan and South Korea co-hosted the 2002 World Cup. This was the first and so far only time the World Cup has been played in two different countries. The opening game was played in Seoul, South Korea, and the final in Japan's 70,000-capacity Yokohama Stadium.

NEW FRONTIERS

Europe and the Americas took turns to host the World Cup between 1958 and 1998, until the first tournament held in Asia in 2002. The first in Africa was held in South Africa in 2010, and organizers are continuing to spread the competition farther afield. Russia, the first Eastern European host, was chosen for the 2018 finals, and the first finals held in the Middle East will be in Qatar in 2022.

▼ *Zabivaka, the official mascot for the 2018 World Cup, is a football-playing wolf. He was chosen by the Russian people in a TV vote.*

43

The World Cup

Only the Summer Olympics comes close to the World Cup as the biggest sporting occasion on the planet. Every four years one nation is crowned the greatest in the world after a tournament usually held in June and July. All eyes will be on Russia in 2018 as the country hosts its first World Cup.

WORLD CUP WINNERS

COUNTRY	WINS	TOURNAMENT YEAR
Brazil	5	1958, 1962, 1970, 1994, 2002
Italy	4	1934, 1938, 1982, 2006
Germany	4	1954, 1974, 1990, 2014
Uruguay	2	1930, 1950
Argentina	2	1978, 1986
England	1	1966
France	1	1998
Spain	1	2010

TROPHIES

The first World Cup trophy, the Jules Rimet Trophy, was stolen just weeks before the 1966 World Cup in England, but was found in South London by a dog named Pickles. His reward was a year's supply of dog food. The trophy was given to Brazil permanently after it won the World Cup for the third time in 1970 but was again stolen in 1983 and has never been found. The current trophy, designed by Italian artist Silvio Gazzaniga, has been used since 1974.

MAJOR UPSETS

Only major football nations have won the World Cup, but there have been plenty of surprise results before the final. One of the biggest shocks came in 1950 when England, appearing at the tournament for the first time, was beaten 1–0 by the USA. Haiti-born Joe Gaetjens scored the only goal. On its first appearance, Senegal defeated holders France 1–0 in the opening match of the 2002 World Cup, while co-host South Korea defeated both Italy and Spain.

◄ *The World Cup Trophy is made of 18-carat gold. It is 36.8 cm tall and weighs 6.1 kg.*

▼ Brazilian forwards Ronaldinho (left) and Rivaldo (right) kiss the World Cup Trophy in 2002. Brazil beat Germany in the final to claim a record fifth title.

SCORING RECORDS

England's Geoff Hurst is the only man to score three goals in a World Cup final. His **hat-trick** helped the host nation beat West Germany 4–2 at Wembley in 1966. The first ever World Cup hat-trick was scored by the USA's Bert Patenaude, in a 3–0 victory over Paraguay in 1930. Oleg Salenko scored a World Cup record five goals in one game, when Russia beat Cameroon 6–1 in 1994.

TOP SCORERS

The Golden Boot is the prize given to the player who scores the most goals at each World Cup tournament. Germany's Miroslav Klose is the competition's all-time top scorer, with 16 goals – five in 2002, five in 2006 when he won the Golden Boot, four in 2010 and two in 2014 when his country won the tournament. No player has scored more goals in one World Cup than Just Fontaine, who scored 13 in 1958, when he helped France finish third.

◄ Striker Just Fontaine played for France from 1953 to 1960, scoring 30 goals in just 21 games for his country.

◄ German striker Miroslav Klose scored a total of 71 goals for his country.

The European Championship

The European Championship was first held in 1960, when the Soviet Union beat Yugoslavia in the final in Paris. It is played every four years, and qualification is open to the 55 countries that are members of UEFA.

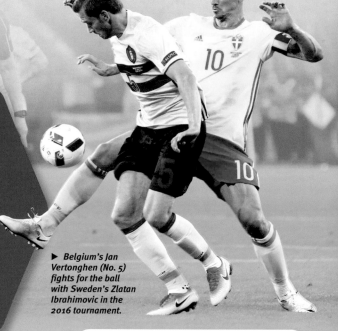

▶ Belgium's Jan Vertonghen (No. 5) fights for the ball with Sweden's Zlatan Ibrahimovic in the 2016 tournament.

FIRST TRIUMPH

Portugal won its first major international trophy by beating host France in the 2016 final. Captain Cristiano Ronaldo was injured early on, but celebrated wildly from the touchline as substitute striker Eder scored the winning goal in extra time. France became the second host nation to lose in the final, after Portugal had itself lost the 2004 final in Lisbon to underdogs Greece.

THE TROPHY

The European Championship trophy is named after French official Henri Delaunay, who came up with the idea of the tournament in 1927 but died five years before the first one was held in 1960. Only four teams qualified for the tournaments from 1960 onwards, before it was expanded to eight teams in 1980, 16 in 1996 and 24 in 2016. The 2020 finals will be held in 13 different cities across Europe, with 24 teams.

▲ The silver Henri Delaunay Trophy is 60 cm tall and weighs 8 kg.

DANISH DELIGHT

Denmark was the surprise winner of the 1992 European Championship in Sweden, despite failing to qualify. It was given a place just 10 days before the tournament began after Yugoslavia withdrew. The Danes beat holders the Netherlands in the semi-final and Germany 2–0 in the final.

Copa América

South America's Copa América is the oldest international football tournament. The first one, held in 1916, was won by Uruguay. It usually features 12 teams – 10 from South America and two guest teams.

PENALTY HEROES

Chile had to wait until 2015 to win its first Copa América, when it beat Argentina on penalties in the final – and it did exactly the same thing the following year, in a special Copa América Centenario to mark 100 years since the first tournament. Goalkeeper and captain Claudio Bravo was the penalty-saving hero both times. The winning penalty in 2015 was scored by Chile's all-time leading goalscorer, Alexis Sánchez.

▲ Uruguay's Martín Cáceres runs clear of Colombia's Juan Cuadrado. Colombia has won the Copa América just once, when it hosted the tournament in 2001.

INVITED GUESTS

Special guests have been invited to take part in the Copa América since 1993, including North American teams Mexico and the USA and teams from further afield such as Japan. The Copa América Centenario in 2016 was played in the USA – the first time the tournament had been held outside South America.

▲ In the Copa América Centenario, Mexico (in green) and Jamaica (in yellow) were both invited guests.

Other international tournaments

Just three teams competed for the first Africa Cup of Nations: Egypt, Ethiopia and Sudan.

48

Every continent has its own football tournament, which takes place in a year without a World Cup. In addition, every four years there is a football tournament for both men and women at the Olympics, where up-and-coming stars have the chance to shine.

OLYMPICS

Britain won the first football tournament at the Summer Olympics, in Paris in 1900. Since 1992 the men's competition has been restricted to under-23s except for three older players per team. Full national teams compete in the women's tournament, which was added to the Games in 1996 and has been won four times by the USA.

▲ Ivory Coast captain Yaya Touré lifts the Africa Cup of Nations trophy in 2015. It was his country's second win.

AFRICA

Africa's international championship, the Africa Cup of Nations, was first played in 1957. Egypt beat Ethiopia 4–0 in the final, and Egypt has now won eight of the 30 tournaments, but the Cup of Nations has more different winners (14) than any other continental championship.

▲ US striker Alex Morgan (right) takes on Japanese defender Saki Kumagai in the 2012 Olympic final in London. The USA won the match 2–1.

ASIA AND OCEANIA

Australia dominated the Oceania OFC Cup before joining the Asian confederation (AFC) in 2005. It won its first AFC Cup in 2015, when midfielder John Troisi scored the winning goal against South Korea. Australia is the only country to be champion of two different continental tournaments.

CONCACAF GOLD CUP

Intense rivalry between the USA and Mexico is guaranteed whenever the CONCACAF Gold Cup is held, every two years. Mexico has won seven titles to its neighbour's six. The USA is the reigning champion, after defeating Jamaica in the 2017 final. Canada is the only other team to have lifted the trophy, in 2001.

Conf d ration-Cup

Every four years, the reigning champions of each continent compete with the World Cup holders and the host nation for the FIFA Confederations Cup. The tournament is held in the country that will stage the following year's World Cup.

◀ The FIFA Confederations Cup trophy.

STARS OF THE FUTURE

Germany won its first FIFA Confederations Cup in Russia in 2017, despite missing many of its senior players, who were given a rest by manager Joachim Löw. Germany's young team was captained by Julian Draxler, aged just 23. He was awarded the Golden Ball for being the tournament's best player, while three-goal teammate Timo Werner won the Golden Boot for top scorer. Germany defeated Chile 1–0 in the final. It was Chile's first appearance in the tournament.

▲ Alexis Sánchez of Chile (left) controls the ball during a match against Germany in the 2017 Confederations Cup.

TREBLE WINNERS

Only three countries have won the FIFA World Cup, the FIFA Confederations Cup and gold at the Summer Olympics: Argentina, France and Brazil, which added its first Olympic gold in 2016. Brazil has won the Confederations Cup a record four times – most recently as host nation in 2013.

◀ The Brazil team celebrates after defeating Spain 3–0 in the 2013 Confederations Cup Final.

The 2013 Confederations Cup was the first tournament to use goal-line technology.

Club teams

The biggest club teams have more followers around the world than national sides. Manchester United, Real Madrid and Barcelona rival each other for the title of richest in the world. All three have a long history of success in international tournaments, but many other clubs have bulging trophy cabinets from domestic triumphs in their own countries.

▲ *Giovanni Trapattoni managed Juventus to victory in all three of Europe's club competitions.*

TRIPLE CROWNS

Only five teams have won all three UEFA club competitions: the European Cup/Champions League, the UEFA Cup/ Europa League and the European Cup Winners' Cup, which ran from 1960 to 1999. These are Juventus (Italy), Ajax (Netherlands), Bayern Munich (Germany), Chelsea and Manchester United (both England). Only Italy has taken all three in the same year: the 1989–90 season ended with AC Milan winning the European Cup, Juventus the UEFA Cup and Sampdoria the European Cup Winners' Cup. This feat can now never be repeated.

▼ *Chelsea players celebrate winning the 2012 Champions League. The team defeated Bayern Munich in the final, held at Bayern's home ground, the Allianz Arena.*

KEY EVENTS

1888
The first ever national football league is organized in England. The title is won by Preston North End, which ends the season unbeaten (see page 58).

1956
Real Madrid defeats Stade de Reims 4–3 in the final of the first European Cup, held in Paris. Real goes on to win the first five cups (see page 52).

1960
The first South American club championship, the Copa Libertadores, is held. It is won by Uruguay's Peñarol (see page 56).

Italian club Lazio was the last team to win the European Cup Winners' Cup in 1999.

HOLLYWOOD GLAMOUR

▶ Landon Donovan scored 113 goals for LA Galaxy between 2005 and 2016.

The club Los Angeles Galaxy was founded at the launch of the United States' Major League Soccer (MLS) in 1996. The club chose its name as a reference to the city's movie stars, and it has certainly been one of the most glamorous US football clubs. LA Galaxy has attracted big names such as England's David Beckham in 2007 and Steven Gerrard in 2015, as well as homegrown hero Landon Donovan, the league's all-time leading goalscorer. It has won a record five MLS Cups.

WEB SUCCESS

Online interaction with fans is becoming increasingly important for football clubs, and is a way of measuring who the most popular club in the world might be. By summer 2017, 105 million had 'liked' Real Madrid's Facebook page and 53.2 million followed it on Instagram. Stars such as Real Madrid's Cristiano Ronaldo and Manchester United's Paul Pogba keep supporters updated with messages, photos and video clips.

LEAGUE LEADERS

Rangers in Scotland has won more domestic league titles than any other club in the world – its most recent title in 2011 was its 54th. Local rival Celtic has won the last six Scottish titles and is currently on 48 titles in total. In Spain, LaLiga has similarly been dominated by its two biggest clubs: Real Madrid with 33 wins, and Barcelona with 24. Belfast club Linfield has dominated Northern Irish domestic football, taking 52 titles, while Peñarol has had similar levels of success in Uruguay, with 48.

▲ Linfield is not a fully professional team, but regularly competes in the Champions League qualifiers as Northern Irish champion.

1992
The European Cup changes its name to the Champions League, expanding to include a group stage before the knock-out rounds (see page 54).

1996
Major League Soccer is launched in the US. It attracts some of the biggest stars in the world (see page 63).

2000
Brazilian club Corinthians wins the first official Club World Cup, beating fellow Brazilians Vasco da Gama in the final (see page 57).

Super clubs

Over the decades, many different clubs have enjoyed periods of success at domestic level and in international competitions. Real Madrid dominated in the 1950s, and has risen to the top again in recent years.

THE REAL THING

Real Madrid won the first five European Cups between 1956 and 1960, helping to establish the competition as Europe's top club prize. The team's star performers were Hungarian striker Ferenc Puskás and Argentina-born Alfredo di Stéfano. Real also recruited French attacker Raymond Kopa after beating his team Stade Reims in the 1956 final. France forward Just Fontaine said: "Apart from Brazil, it was the best team I ever saw."

▲ Real Madrid striker Alfredo Di Stéfano was a powerful forward who could start attacks from deep in defence.

TOURING STARS

Brazilian club Santos became South American champions in 1962 and 1963 and also beat the best Europe had to offer in the Club World Cup. The team from São Paulo's leading attraction was Pelé, but it featured seven other World Cup-winning Brazilians. The team played such entertaining football, it was invited to tour the world playing **friendlies** against other clubs.

◀ Pelé joined Santos as a 15-year-old, and stayed for the next 18 years.

EUROPEAN FORCES

Several clubs have dominated the European Cup for short periods. Dutch club Ajax won the trophy three times in a row from 1971 to 1973, playing the fluid style called Total Football. West Germany's Bayern Munich won a hat-trick of titles from 1974 to 1976, then English club Liverpool won the Cup four times between 1977 and 1984. Italy's AC Milan took the tournament in 1988 and 1989, led by the Dutch trio Ruud Gullit, Marco van Basten and Frank Rijkaard.

Real Madrid's first European Cup goal was scored by its captain Miguel Muñoz in 1955.

MANCHESTER UNITED

In 1958, a plane carrying a young Manchester United squad to Munich airport crashed, killing eight of the players. Ten years later, led by crash survivors captain Bobby Charlton and manager Matt Busby, the Red Devils became the first English club to win the European Cup. Charlton formed a prolific forward partnership with George Best and Denis Law, known as the United Trinity, as the team beat Benfica 4–1 in the final.

▼ *Statue of the United Trinity outside Old Trafford stadium.*

▶ *Honvéd FC played English champions Wolverhampton Wanderers in a friendly in 1954, a year before the start of the European Cup.*

BUDAPEST HONVÉD

In 1949, the Hungarian army took over the Budapest club Kispest FC, renaming it Budapest Honvéd. They raided the top players from rival teams to create what was effectively a practice squad for the Hungarian national team. It had some of the best players of the day, such as star strikers Ferenc Puskás and Sándor Kocsi. Nicknamed the 'Magical Magyars', the team established itself as the dominant force in European club football in the early 1950s.

▲ *English star forward Kevin Keegan played for Hamburg from 1977 to 1980. He was the highest-paid player in Germany.*

HAMBURGER SV

Hamburg was the dominant force in German football from 1976 to 1983, when it won three league titles and the European Cup. This talented team was led by star midfielder Felix Magath, and managed by the Austrian Ernst Happel. Magath scored the winning goal in the final of the 1983 European Cup, which was his last match as a professional footballer.

The Champion- League

Europe's premier club tournament was known as the European Cup until 1992, when it changed its name to the Champions League. The competition pits many of the biggest clubs in the world against one another for the crown of champion of champions.

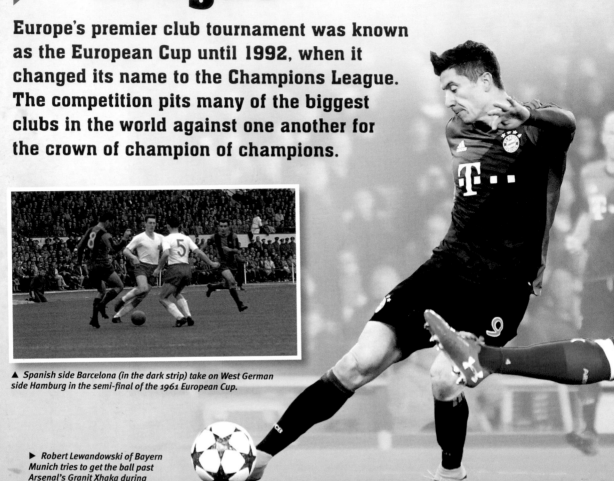

▲ Spanish side Barcelona (in the dark strip) take on West German side Hamburg in the semi-final of the 1961 European Cup.

▶ Robert Lewandowski of Bayern Munich tries to get the ball past Arsenal's Granit Xhaka during a Champions League game in 2017.

RECORD HOLDERS

There were several unofficial European club competitions before the first European Cup tournament was organized in 1955–56. The Spanish champion Real Madrid was the tournament's first winner, beating French team Stade de Reims 4–3. Real won the first five tournaments, and has now won it a record 12 times, including in 2017, when its star striker Cristiano Ronaldo scored twice in a 4–1 victory over Italian club Juventus.

CHAMPIONS LEAGUE CHANGES

Since 1992, the main first round of the tournament has consisted of eight groups of four teams, which all play each other home and away. The top two from each group qualify for the knockout rounds. Up to 1992, only the league champions from each country qualified. Today, the teams finishing second, third and even fourth from leading nations, such as England, Spain, Germany and Italy, can qualify.

Two managers have won the European Cup three times: Liverpool's Bob Paisley in 1977, 1978 and 1981, and Carlo Ancelotti with AC Milan in 2003 and 2007 and with Real Madrid in 2014. Only one player has won with three different clubs: Dutch midfielder Clarence Seedorf, with Ajax in 1995, Real Madrid in 1998 and AC Milan in 2003 and 2007.

HIGH SCORERS

The fifth European Cup Final in 1960 was the highest-scoring of all time, when Spain's Real Madrid beat Germany's Eintracht Frankfurt 7–3. Two other clubs have won the final by four goals: Bayern Munich, 4–0 against Atletico Madrid in 1974, and AC Milan, 4–0 against Steaua Bucharest in 1989, and by the same score against Barcelona five years later. The biggest margin of victory in any European Cup match was when Romania's Dinamo Bucharest beat Northern Ireland's Crusaders 11–0 in the first round in 1973.

▲ *Portuguese ace Cristiano Ronaldo is the leading scorer in the Champions League, with a total of 105 goals for Manchester United and Real Madrid by the end of the 2016–17 season.*

ENGLISH ERA

Between 1977 and 1982, English clubs dominated the European Cup winning all six titles. Three different clubs lifted the trophy: Liverpool (three times), Nottingham Forest (twice) and Aston Villa. Liverpool went on to win a fourth title in 1984, but the English era came to an end in 1985 when English clubs were banned from playing in European competitions for five years due to hooliganism.

◄ *Liverpool captain Emlyn Hughes lifts the trophy after victory over German side Borussia Mönchengladbach in 1977.*

Other Champions' leagues

The success of the European Cup has inspired similar competitions across the world. Today, each continent's top club teams compete every year in their own version of the Champions League.

COPA LIBERTADORES

The South American club championship began in 1960, when the league winners from each country across the continent were invited to take part. Uruguayan side Peñarol won the first two tournaments, with Alberto Spencer scoring the winning goals both times. His 54 goals remain a Copa Libertadores record. Argentina's Independiente has won the trophy a record seven times.

▲ *Universidad Católica of Chile (in blue and white) takes on Brazilian team Flamengo at Flamengo's home ground, the Maracanã in Rio de Janeiro.*

AFRICA, ASIA AND OCEANIA

Asia's AFC Champions League was founded in 1967, and has been won most by South Korean club Pohang Steelers, with three titles. Egyptian side Al Ahly has triumphed a record eight times in the African competition, the CAF Champions League, which began in 1964. Auckland City from New Zealand lifted Oceania's OFC Champions League for a record ninth time in 2017.

◄ *The Qatari Al Sadd team celebrates after winning the AFC Champions League trophy for the second time in 2011.*

The Copa Libertadores trophy carries the badges of each team that wins on its pedestal.

Club World Cup

The FIFA Club World Cup is a contest between the reigning club champions of each continent: Europe, South America, North America, Africa, Asia and Oceania (the Pacific Islands). They are joined by the domestic champion of the host nation.

▲ FIFA World Club Cup trophy.

DOMINATION

The first official Club World Cup was held in 2000 and was won on penalties by Brazilian club Corinthians against another Brazilian side, Vasco da Gama. The tournament has continued to be dominated by South American and European clubs, with three victories for Barcelona, two for Corinthians and two for Real Madrid. Corinthians' winning team in 2012 included Danilo and Fabio Santos, who had both won the tournament in 2005 with São Paulo.

▲ Corinthians players celebrate their second Club World Cup victory in 2012 after beating European champions Chelsea in the final.

◀ Kashima Antlers' Mu Kanazaki wins the ball from Real Madrid's Raphael Varane in the 2016 final.

SURPRISE CHALLENGERS

The first club outside Europe and South America to reach a Club World Cup final was the Democratic Republic of Congo's TP Mazembe in 2010, which lost the final 3–0 to Internazionale from Italy. In the 2016 final, held in Japan, the Japanese champions Kashima Antlers led Real Madrid after an hour 2–1, with two goals by Gabu Shibusaki. But a Cristiano Ronaldo hat-trick helped the Spaniards win 4–2 after the match had gone into extra time.

English league

In 2004, Arsenal won the Premier League title without losing a single match all season.

58

The first organized national football league was started in England in 1888 to provide teams with a series of guaranteed matches each year. Today, England's prestigious Premier League sits above three lower fully professional national divisions.

FIRST DIVISION

There were 12 teams in the first English league season, including current Premier League clubs Burnley, Everton, Stoke City and West Bromwich Albion. As it grew in popularity, new divisions were added. The English Premier League was formed in 1992, replacing the old First Division.

NORTHERN POWERHOUSES

The two most successful English clubs, Liverpool and Manchester United, are both based in north-west England. In 1968, United was the first English team to win the European Cup, coached by former Liverpool player Sir Matt Busby. It has won the tournament twice more, in 1999 and 2008, and has won the English league a record 20 times. Liverpool took the last of its 18 league titles in 1990, but it has won the European Cup/Champions League five times.

◄ *Sir Alex Ferguson won a record 13 league titles with Manchester United between 1986 and 2013, becoming the Premier League's most-successful manager.*

DOUBLING UP

Winning both the English league and the FA Cup in the same season is known as 'the Double'. Preston North End, which won the first league championship in 1889, won the first Double that same year. Aston Villa repeated this achievement in 1897. Tottenham Hotspur was the first Double-winner of the 20th century in 1961. Arsenal and Manchester United have both won the Double three times.

▲ *Preston North End won the first English league title. The league only contained teams from the Midlands and the north-west region of England.*

Spain's LaLiga

Spain's top division, known worldwide as 'LaLiga', started in 1929. It is officially ranked Europe's strongest league by UEFA, and the continent's top-rated club has come from Spain a record 20 times.

EL CLÁSICO

LaLiga is dominated by Spain's two biggest clubs – arch-rivals Barcelona and Real Madrid. Games between the two are known as 'El Clásico', and attract huge crowds. Real has won LaLiga 33 times, and Barcelona 24 times.
Both teams contain some of the greatest attacking players in the world. Real has Cristiano Ronaldo, Gareth Bale and Karim Benzema, while Barcelona boasts Lionel Messi and Luis Suárez.

▲ *Gareth Bale of Real Madrid and Sergio Busquets of Barcelona compete for the ball in an El Clásico fixture.*

PLAYER PRIZES

The prize for the top goalscorer in Spain each year is called the 'Pichichi', after the Athletic Bilbao striker Rafael 'Pichichi' Moreno. Since 2010, it has been won four times by Lionel Messi, three times by Cristiano Ronaldo and once by Luis Suárez. The award for the goalkeeper who keeps the most **clean sheets** is called the 'Zamora', after former Espanyol, Barcelona and Real Madrid goalkeeper Ricardo Zamora.

▼ *Barcelona's Lionel Messi scored a LaLiga record of 50 goals in the 2010–11 season.*

Other European leagues

During the 20th century, a number of professional football leagues were formed across Europe, and many of them now feature some of the world's best-known clubs. Germany's Bundesliga attracts the biggest crowds, with an average attendance of 40,000 people per match across the league.

▶ *Ajax's Piet Keizer (right) collects the ball during the 1972 European Cup Final. Ajax won the competition three times in a row from 1971 to 1973.*

▲ *Johan Cruyff, Ajax's greatest player.*

THE DUTCH BIG THREE

The Dutch league, known as the Eredivisie, has been the training ground for some of the world's most gifted footballers. During the 1970s, Amsterdam club Ajax became famous for its stylish football, centred around the genius of forward Johan Cruyff. Ajax's biggest rivals for the Eredivisie title are Feyenoord from Rotterdam and PSV from Eindhoven.

TURKISH DELIGHTS

Only five clubs have won the Turkish league championship, the Super Lig, since it started in 1958, and three of them are from the city of Istanbul. Galatasaray leads the way with 20 titles, followed by city rivals Fenerbahce (19) and Besiktas (15). Trabzonspor, from Trabzon, won the last of its six titles in 1984, while Bursaspor, from Bursa, secured its only championship title in 2010.

With an average crowd of 80,000, Borussia Dortmund is the best-supported club in the world.

ITALIAN ICONS

A team called Ambrosiana won Italy's first national league title in 1930. Later the club reverted to its original name Internazionale, or Inter Milan. The team was formed by a split with its city rivals, now known as AC Milan. Italy's most successful side, however, is Juventus, based in the city of Turin. Juventus has won Serie A, the top division of Italian football, a record 33 times. The two Milan teams are next on the list with 18 titles each.

PRESENTI ANTONIO CON NOI

UD MILA

▲ *AC Milan fans spread their flags across the seats of the San Siro, the massive stadium that the club shares with rivals Inter Milan.*

FRENCH SPENDING

The top division in France, Ligue 1, is home to Brazilian Neymar, who became the world's most expensive football player when he left Barcelona for Paris Saint-Germain (PSG) for £198 million in August 2017. PSG was only formed in 1970, but it has already won 33 trophies – more than any other French club. It has six league titles, although it is still behind Saint-Etienne (ten), Marseille (nine), and Nantes and Monaco (eight each).

NEYMAR JR
10

GERMAN DOMINANCE

Germany was later than many major European nations in starting its own national and professional top football division. The Bundesliga began in 1963, after many decades of regional competitions. Bayern Munich did not reach the top division until two years later, but it has since become the dominant club. Its main challengers have been Borussia Mönchengladbach in the 1970s, Hamburg in the 1980s and, more recently, Borussia Dortmund. Bayern won the Bundesliga in 2017 for the fifth year running.

◀ *Bayern Munich's star French forward Franck Ribéry shields the ball from Chelsea's André Schürrle during a UEFA Super Cup match.*

Leagues around the world

São Paulo goalkeeper Rogério Ceni took free kicks and ended his career with 129 goals.

62

The first league competitions outside Britain appeared in South America. Today, the MLS in North America is among the fastest-growing leagues, while similar tournaments are expanding around the globe thanks to extra investment and increased media coverage.

◀ Gabriel Franco of Botafogo (in black and white) competes for the ball with Lucas Lima of Santos during a Brazil Cup match at the Maracanã Stadium in Rio de Janeiro.

SOUTH AMERICA

The first league championship organized outside Britain began in Argentina in 1891. In the capital Buenos Aires, games between city rivals River Plate and Boca Juniors are known as the 'Superclásico', and the atmosphere at these matches is well known as among the most passionate in the world. A national league has only been running in Brazil since 1971. The Campeonato Brasileiro has been won by 17 different clubs and the most successful club is Palmeiras, which has won the league nine times.

▲ Argentinian star Juan Román Riquelme started his career at Boca Juniors.

ASIA

Japan's first professional league, the J. League, was launched in 1993 with 10 clubs and star signings such as Brazil's Zico, England's Gary Lineker and Italy's Toto Schillaci. It now has 18 clubs, including 2016 champions Kashima Antlers, which has won a record eight J. League titles. Winners qualify for the annual AFC Champions League, featuring clubs from across Asia, including the Chinese Super League.

▲ Japan's Kashima Antlers (in the dark kit) takes on Thai champions Muangthong United in the 2017 AFC Champions League.

▲ Kaizer Chiefs players celebrate their league win in 2015. Based in Soweto, it is South Africa's best-supported team.

NORTH AMERICA

The USA struggled for many years to establish a national league. The NASL, or North American Soccer League, ran from 1968 to 1984. Major League Soccer (MLS) was launched in 1996 and features 22 teams from the USA and Canada. Star MLS players have included England's David Beckham, Ireland's Robbie Keane, America's Landon Donovan, Italy's Andrea Pirlo and Spain's David Villa.

▶ England's David Beckham on the ball while playing for LA Galaxy. The team sold 250,000 of his number 23 shirts before Beckham even arrived in the USA.

AFRICA

South Africa established its first proper professional league in 1996, and in 2016 Mamelodi Sundowns became the first South African team to win the African Champions League. Over the years, this competition has been dominated by the Egyptian clubs Al Ahly and Zamalek, which have won it 13 times between them.

Pl..a..nd players

Everyone will have their own favourites, but there are certain footballers and venues that have made more impact than most – and provided some of the game's most memorable achievements and occasions.

▲ *An estimated 110,000 people crammed into Crystal Palace in south London to watch the 1901 FA Cup Final.*

GROUNDS APPEAL

Venues can vary from huge and stunning arenas to basic local grounds. English football began in the 19th century on open fields, with barely any seating or stands, often on cricket fields such as The Oval in Kennington, south London, where many of the first internationals were played. Bramall Lane in Sheffield, England, is believed to be the oldest ground still in use for football matches. It opened in 1855 primarily for cricket, and staged its first game of football in 1862.

▲ *Built in 1892, Everton's Goodison Park in Liverpool was the world's first purpose-built football stadium.*

KEY EVENTS

1923
Wembley Stadium in London hosts its first match, the FA Cup Final. It is estimated that more than 200,000 people squeezed in (see page 66).

1953
Hungary thrashes England twice in the space of six months – first in London and then in Budapest (see page 68).

1986
Argentina wins the World Cup, inspired by Diego Maradona, who scores an amazing solo goal in the quarter-final against England (see page 69).

PRIZES FOR PLAYERS

The Ballon d'Or (meaning 'Golden Ball') is a prize for the best player of the year decided by Paris magazine *France Football*. It was first awarded in 1956 and was initially limited to European players, but has been open to all nationalities since 2007. It has been won five times by both Lionel Messi and Cristiano Ronaldo. FIFA also presents awards: the Best FIFA Men's Player 2017 was Portugal's Cristiano Ronaldo, while the Best FIFA Women's Player prize went to Lieke Martens of the Netherlands.

▲ The Ballon d'Or trophy is a gold-plated ball that is 23 cm in diameter.

OLDEST CLUB

Nottingham is home to the oldest professional football club still in existence. Notts County currently plays in the fourth tier of English football. The club was formed in 1862, one year before the Football Association produced the first set of laws, and initially played according to rules of its own creation. It was a founding member of the Football League in 1888, but the club has struggled to make a major impact since the 1920s.

▲ The 1894 FA Cup-winning Notts County team poses for a photo. This win remains the club's only major domestic trophy.

2004
US striker Mia Hamm ends her 17-year career with 158 international goals, a then-record for any player male or female (see page 71).

2016
Cristiano Ronaldo wins his first international honour by leading Portugal to the European Championship (see page 73).

2017
Dutch striker Vivianne Miedema scores twice in the European Women's Championship final as the Netherlands beats Denmark 4–2 (see page 75).

Stadiums

Football stadiums around the world have become famous for their size, their style or the historic games that have been played there. The best stadiums of all create a cauldron of noise as the fans cheer on their teams.

▲ *The 92,500-capacity Rose Bowl was built in 1922. As well as football matches, it has hosted the American football Super Bowl five times.*

UNIQUE TREBLE

The Rose Bowl in Pasadena, California, is the only stadium to host a men's World Cup final (when Brazil beat Italy in 1994), a Women's World Cup final (when the USA beat China in 1999) and an Olympic final (when France beat Brazil in 1984). The Rose Bowl is most often used for American football, or gridiron.

WEMBLEY

Built in 1923, Wembley Stadium in London has been called 'the home of football'. The original stadium staged many major events, including the 1966 World Cup Final and three European Cup finals, before it was knocked down in 2002. The new stadium features a 133-metre-tall arch that can be seen across the city. The new stadium opened in 2007 and is set to host the 2020 European Championship Final.

THE MARACANÃ

▲ *The modernized Maracanã has a capacity of 79,000.*

The Maracanã Stadium in the Brazilian city of Rio de Janeiro was opened in 1950. That year, it hosted the final game of the 1950 World Cup, in which Brazil lost 2–1 to Uruguay. Nearly 175,000 spectators were crammed in. A modernized stadium with a much-reduced capacity hosted the World Cup Final in 2014, when Germany beat Argentina 1–0. Two years later, Brazil won Olympic Gold at the stadium by defeating Germany on penalties, with Neymar scoring the winning goal.

ALLIANZ ARENA

The 75,000-capacity Allianz Arena in Munich is home to German giant Bayern Munich. Opened in 2005, the stadium is nicknamed the 'inflatable boat' after the air-filled panels that surround its outer facade. The panels are lit up in different colours depending on the home team: red for Bayern Munich and white for the German national team.

▼ *The Allianz Arena is lit up red, showing that Bayern Munich is playing at home.*

▼ *The 90,000-seat Wembley Stadium features a sliding roof that keeps the whole crowd dry in bad weather.*

▲ *The 95,000-capacity Soccer City is located in Soweto, Johannesburg. It is the home ground of the Kaizer Chiefs club.*

SOCCER CITY

The FNB Stadium, also known as 'Soccer City', in the South African city of Johannesburg is the only stadium in Africa to stage a World Cup final. In the 2010 tournament, Spain defeated the Netherlands 1–0 at Soccer City. Former South African president Nelson Mandela toured the pitch in a golf cart before the game kicked off. The venue was designed to look like a cooking pot known as a calabash. Holes in the sides allow lights to flicker through.

Great games

Certain matches have gone down in history for their thrilling action or the unexpected result. How fans feel about these classic games depends very much on which team they support.

▼ Hungary's 1953 team, nicknamed the 'Golden Team'.

ITALY 4 WEST GERMANY 3

In the 1970 World Cup semi-final in Mexico, Italy won after extra time. It was 1–1 at the end of normal time after the Germans had equalized in the last minute. Then five goals were scored in a thrilling extra 30 minutes. Italy went on to lose 4–1 in the final to a strong Brazil team.

ENGLAND 3 HUNGARY 6

England's first ever home defeat to a non-British team was a 6–3 loss to Hungary at Wembley in 1953. Hungary's captain Ferenc Puskás scored two and Nandor Hidegkuti hit a hat-trick. To prove it was no fluke, Hungary thrashed England again six months later in Budapest, winning 7–1.

▼ Gerd Müller (in the white shirt) equalized for West Germany, only for Italy to score the winner less than a minute later.

BRAZIL 1 GERMANY 7

This 2014 World Cup semi-final was one of football's most startling scorelines. Host Brazil, missing its injured star striker Neymar, had its dreams of a home World Cup triumph destroyed in the first half as the visitors scored five goals in half an hour. Five different German players scored in the match, in front of disbelieving fans in the Mineirão Stadium, Belo Horizonte. Germany went on to beat Argentina in the final. The Brazilian nation went into shock.

◄ Sami Khedira (in red and black) scored Germany's fifth goal in its shock win over Brazil.

Wonder goals

It takes only a few seconds to score a goal, but some goals are so spectacular that they will be remembered forever. Even with regular goalscorers, such as Diego Maradona and Marco van Basten, there is one goal that stands above all the others.

MARADONA'S MAGIC

Diego Maradona's second goal for Argentina against England in the 1986 World Cup quarter-final was voted the greatest World Cup goal of all time in a poll in 2002. He dribbled the ball all the way from just inside his own half before nudging it past goalkeeper Peter Shilton. Maradona scored a similar goal in the semi-final and lifted the trophy for Argentina as an inspirational captain.

◄ In the 1986 World Cup quarter-final, Argentina's Diego Maradona beat five England defenders and the goalkeeper before calmly placing the ball in the net.

LONG-RANGE SHOTS AND VOLLEYS

◄ The USA's Carli Lloyd celebrates after scoring her spectacular third goal in the 2015 Women's World Cup Final.

Powerful long-range shots that rocket into the top corner of the net are among the most spectacular goals. Some players have even scored with shots from inside their own half: Spain's Xabi Alonso did so twice for Liverpool. One of Carli Lloyd's hat-trick goals for the USA against Japan in the 2015 Women's World Cup Final was struck from the halfway line. Volleying the ball into the net takes power and technique. One of the best was Marco van Basten's angled volley, after a long pass across the pitch from Arnold Muhren, as the Netherlands beat the Soviet Union 2–0 in the 1988 European Championship final.

In 1996, David Beckham scored for Manchester United with a shot from his own half.

The best players

Arguments will continue as to who was the best player ever, but here are some of the undisputed greats of the game. They lit up the pitch with their individual skill and style, and led their teams to glory.

▲ Pelé combined speed and power with technical ability and the vision to pick out a cross that nobody else had seen.

▼ With his low centre of gravity and sublime balance, it was almost impossible to take the ball from Maradona's feet.

PELÉ

Edson Arantes do Nascimento, better known as Pelé, is the only man to win three World Cups. This started with a string of amazing performances as a 17-year-old at the 1958 tournament, where he scored twice in the 5–2 final win over Sweden. Pelé was good with both feet and a prolific goalscorer, scoring more than 1000 goals for Brazil and his club side Santos. Later in his career, he played in the USA, helping to popularize the sport there.

DIEGO MARADONA

Argentinian Diego Maradona is the man most often mentioned alongside Pelé as the greatest ever player. With a magical left foot, he terrorized defenders with his dazzling dribbling skills and scored many outstanding goals. Maradona's attacking threat carried an ordinary Argentina team to World Cup glory in 1986, and he also inspired outsiders Napoli to two Serie A title wins in Italy.

MIA HAMM

An athletic and technically gifted striker, Mia Hamm broke many records in her long career for the USA women's team. She won two Olympic Golds and two World Cups in her 17-year international career, scoring 158 international goals in 276 appearances. At club level, Hamm was a founding player in the USA's first professional league. She played for the club Washington Freedom and became one of the best-known sportspeople in the country.

▶ *Mia Hamm was a versatile forward who could play up front or drop back to deeper positions.*

▲ *Johan Cruyff (centre) never won the World Cup. His team was the favourite in 1974, but lost in the final to West Germany.*

JOHAN CRUYFF

Dutch forward Johan Cruyff helped to create a new style of football in the 1970s. He played for Ajax and Barcelona, as well as the Dutch national team, at a time when players were being encouraged to fill any position – the style called 'Total Football'. He was tall and skilful and came up with a move now known as the 'Cruyff turn' at the 1974 World Cup, beating defenders by dragging the ball backwards between his own legs.

GEORGE BEST

Admirers of Manchester United and Northern Ireland's George Best would often use the slogan "Pelé good, Maradona better, George Best". With his risk-taking dribbling style, Best helped United to its first European Cup in 1968, but he never had the opportunity to display his dazzling skills at a World Cup. Off the field, Best was one of the first celebrity footballers, known for his extravagant lifestyle and tastes.

▶ *George Best played international football for Northern Ireland, but the team did not qualify for any major finals during his career.*

Modern icons

Today's best footballers are regarded by many as among the finest of all time. Lionel Messi and Cristiano Ronaldo are established stars, having dominated the game for a decade. Other major talents may have their most successful years still ahead of them as the game's top stars get fitter and faster than ever before.

▲ *Small and slight, Messi has great balance on the ball and unmatched close control.*

LIONEL MESSI

Lionel Messi has won the Ballon d'Or five times, an achievement he shares with Cristiano Ronaldo. He left his home country of Argentina at the age of 13 to join Spanish side Barcelona, for whom he has played his entire career. Naturally left-footed, Messi's brilliant dribbling and shooting have helped Barcelona win the Champions League four times. He was voted the best player at the 2014 World Cup, even though Argentina lost in the final to Germany.

NEYMAR

Alongside Argentina's Lionel Messi and Uruguay's Luis Suárez, Brazilian Neymar completed an incredible attacking trio for Barcelona. In 2016, he was Brazil's captain and the winning goalscorer when the team won Olympic Gold on home soil. In 2017, he left Barcelona for France's Paris Saint-Germain for a world record £198 million (222 million euros) transfer fee.

▶ Seen here playing for Brazil in 2013, Neymar has a range of dazzling tricks up his sleeve and can control the ball equally well with both feet.

CRISTIANO RONALDO

Tall and powerful, Portuguese star Ronaldo began his career at Sporting CP and then Manchester United as a winger. However, his strength and heading skills have helped him become more of a centre forward in recent years. He has been a prolific scorer since moving to Real Madrid in 2009. He has a fearsome shot with either foot and is renowned for his free kicks. Ronaldo went off injured early in the 2016 European Championship final but still lifted the trophy as Portugal won the game.

▲ Cristiano Ronaldo celebrates a goal for Real Madrid in typical style. He combines skill and speed with an intimidating physical presence.

GARETH BALE

Welshman Gareth Bale began his career in defence, but developed into a powerful left winger and regular goalscorer, often shooting from long range. He joined Real Madrid in 2013, and helped them to three Champions League titles in the next four seasons. Bale starred for Wales as it reached the semi-finals of the 2016 European Championship.

▶ Gareth Bale in action for Real Madrid.

Women to watch

Women's football is enjoying ever-growing exposure across the world, and millions now tune in for the big games. Many top stars play for Europe's leading clubs or in the US professional league.

◀ *Alex Morgan played for the Portland Thorns from 2013 to 2015, but has since moved to the Orlando Pride.*

ALEX MORGAN

USA striker Alex Morgan has become renowned for scoring late goals. At the 2012 Summer Olympics in London, she scored the winner in the semi-final against France in the 123rd minute: three minutes into **stoppage time** added at the end of extra time. She set up one of Carli Lloyd's two winning goals in the final against Japan. Morgan finished 2012 with a phenomenal 28 international goals.

LUCY BRONZE

England's Lucy Bronze mainly plays in defence, but she is a versatile player who can also operate in midfield. She popped up in attack to score the winning goal for Manchester City in the 2016 Women's FA Cup Final at Wembley. Bronze was a regular for England when reaching the semi-finals at both the 2015 Women's World Cup and the 2017 Women's European Championship. In 2017, she moved to the top French club Olympique Lyonnaise, the current holders of the Women's Champions League.

◀ *Lucy Bronze has played for several clubs, including a two-year stint at Liverpool.*

Sam Kerr scored four goals as Sky Blue FC recovered from 3–0 down to beat Seattle in 2017.

◀ *At 24 years old, Sam Kerr has already won more than 50 caps for Australia.*

VIVIANNE MIEDEMA

Vivianne Miedema is a prolific striker for both the Netherlands and at club level, and has been praised for a 'killer instinct' in front of goal by her national coach Roger Reigners. She scored twice for the Dutch in their 4–2 victory over Denmark in the 2017 UEFA European Championship Final. That game took her to 45 goals in only 57 international appearances, at the age of just 21.

▶ *Vivianne Miedema is an out-and-out striker with a knack for scoring in big games.*

SAM KERR

Australian forward Sam Kerr played her first international match at the age of just 15 in 2009. She is now one of the major stars of the USA's National Women's Soccer League, playing for New Jersey's Sky Blue FC. She was top scorer at the Tournament Of Nations, a competition played for the first time in 2017 between Australia, Brazil, Japan and the USA.

▶ *Leroux switched from Canada to the USA in order to test herself at the highest level.*

SYDNEY LEROUX

Born in Canada to a Canadian mother and an American father, striker Sydney Leroux wanted to play for the USA national side from a young age. She switched her national allegiance to the USA in 2008. She has been a regular in the USA national side since 2011, and was the youngest member of the 2012 Olympic Gold medal-winning squad. By 2017, she had scored 35 goals in 77 appearances.

Strange but true

Football is big business, but there can be a lighter side to even the biggest of occasions, sometimes accidentally. Kits, animals and eccentric locations all add to the entertainment of the sporting experience.

UNUSUAL KITS

Manager Alex Ferguson ordered his Manchester United players to change out of their all-grey away kit at half-time against Southampton in 1997, blaming their poor play on finding it hard to see each other. Cameroon tried a one-piece shirt-and-shorts kit in 2004, but it was banned by FIFA and the Cameroon federation was fined. France played a first-round game at the 1978 World Cup in the green and white stripes of local Argentine club Atletico Kimberley after arriving with a white kit to play Hungary, who were also wearing white. The Dutch club Heerenveen has red love-hearts between their blue and white stripes.

Hungary's away kit

France's official away kit

France's kit for the day

▲ *France and Hungary both turned up in their white away shirts for their match in the 1978 World Cup. Kick-off was delayed for an hour while different shirts were found for the French team to wear.*

ANIMAL MAGIC

An octopus named Paul became famous during the 2010 World Cup in Germany when he successfully predicted eight results by choosing a box of food to eat with the right team's name next to it. During the 1962 World Cup, a dog ran onto the pitch in Chile and was finally caught by England player Jimmy Greaves. Opposing player Garrincha, from Brazil, adopted the dog as a pet.

◄ *Paul in his tank in 2010.*

UNUSUAL STADIUMS

One of the most dramatic football stadiums in the world is the home ground of Portuguese club Braga, whose stadium was built into cliffs. It was one of the venues for the 2004 European Championship. A stadium in Singapore called The Float is built on a floating platform in the sea, while Belgrade's Stadion Vozdovac is on top of a shopping centre. Trains run through Slovakian team TJ Tatran Cierny Balog's small ground, which only holds 480 fans.

▲ Also known as 'The Quarry', the Municipal Stadium in Braga was carved out of the face of Monte do Castro. The stadium was built in 2003.

◄ The Float at Marina Bay in Singapore is supported by six pylons that are fixed to the harbour floor.

GLOSSARY

CAP

An international appearance by a player for their country.

CLEAN SHEET

A game in which a goalkeeper or team does not concede a goal.

CONFEDERATION

One of the organizations that oversees football on a continent. There are six of these confederations, including UEFA in Europe and CAF in Africa.

CORNER

A kick taken by the attacking team, within one yard of the corner flag, if a defending player was the last to touch the ball before it went behind the goal line.

DRIBBLING

When a player runs with the ball at their feet, keeping it under close control and nudging it forwards with small kicks.

EXTRA TIME

An extra period of 30 minutes play, split between two 15-minute halves, added on at the end of a cup tie's 90 minutes if the score remains level.

FOUL

When one player unfairly trips, kicks, blocks or otherwise attacks an opponent. This is punished with a free kick against the guilty party or a penalty if the foul occurs inside the penalty area.

FREE KICK

A free shot or pass, taken from a stationary position. It is given against players if they break any laws of the game such as fouls, handball or offside. Players facing a free kick must be at least ten yards away.

FRIENDLY

A game which is not part of a league or cup competition.

GOAL

A goal is scored when the whole of the ball crosses the goal line between the goalposts and under the crossbar. The team scoring the most goals during a match wins.

GOAL LINE

The line at each end of the pitch running right across the field between the two corner flags.

HANDBALL

When someone who is not the goalkeeper deliberately touches the ball with their hands or arms.

HAT-TRICK

Three goals scored in the same game by the same player.

IMMIGRANT

A person who travels from one region or country to another in order to live and work.

OFFSIDE

When a player in their opponent's half receives the ball after it has been passed forwards and only has fewer than two opposing players between the ball and the goal. The defending team receives a free kick.

PENALTY

A free shot, from the penalty spot 11 metres from goal, given to an attacking team if they are the victims of a foul or handball inside the defending team's rectangular penalty area.

PENALTY SHOOT-OUT

A method of settling a drawn game in cup competitions, with each team taking turns to take a penalty. If they remain level after five each, they continue until one scores and the other misses.

QUALIFIER

A match played in the run-up to a tournament. It decides which teams should appear at the tournament itself.

RED CARD

This is shown to players who are dismissed from the field and cannot be replaced nor come back on for the rest of the game. They can be shown a red card for offences such as dangerous fouling or violent conduct, or if they are shown a second yellow card.

REFEREE

The official in charge of starting, ending and controlling the match, punishing players for breaking the laws and giving permission for substitutions. He or she is helped by assistant referees on the two touchlines, and a fourth official watching from off the pitch.

SOCCER

A shortening of 'association football', football is known as soccer in some parts of the world, such as the USA.

STOPPAGE TIME

Also called injury time, these are extra minutes added to the end of a half to make up for time lost during stoppages such as substitutions, injuries or goals.

SUBSTITUTE

Players who do not start the game but can be brought on, whether for tactical reasons or if the player they are replacing is injured.

TIKI-TAKA

The name given to a style of playing that involves short passes between teammates. It was made popular by the Spanish national team and Barcelona in the first decade of the 21st century.

TRANSFER

A move between clubs by a player, often with the buying side paying a sum of money to the selling team.

INDEX

Picture credits (t=top, b=bottom, l=left, r=right, c=centre, fc=front cover, bc=back cover) All images are from Dreamstime.com, except: Alamy: 10c Art Collection 2, 12c Andrea Spinelli, 13t ZUMA Press, Inc., 16c, 28cl dpa picture alliance archive, 23b Newscom, 24b Interfoto, 25t G. Loinaz, 36 United Archives GmbH, 38b Action Plus Sports Images, 44–45 Allstar Picture Library, 49cr Newscom, 53c Black Country Images, 53b Werner Otto, 57b Aflo Co. Ltd. Getty Images: 55b Bob Thomas. Shutterstock: 24t, 25b, 40, 59t, 61tl, 63t. Creative Commons Attribution/Sharealike: fc line 3r Steindy, 15t Football.ua, 17bl MDBR, 18b MCaviglia, 21t Little Savage, 28t Kieran Clarke, 33t Agência Brasil Fotografias, 33b, 41b Ailura, 37Rodrigo Gómez Sanz, 42c Yumemi.K, 46b Kirill Venediktov, 48tr Wikimedia, 48cl Ben Sutherland, 49tl Frolzart, 51t Regular Daddy, 52bl Bilsen, Joop van/Anefo, 54tl Harry Pot, 56b Doha Stadium Plus Qatar, 57c Tomofumi Kitano, 58tl Austin Osuide, 6ot Kroon, Ron/Anefo, 60b Bert Verhoeff Nationaal Archief, 74bl joshjdss, 75tl Ann Odong, 75b Noah Salzman, 76t Tilla, 77c Forgemind ArchiMedia